A Certain Time

GARETH BUCKETT

New Prospect Press

Published by New Prospect Press
www.newprospectart.co.uk

Printed and bound by

Image Digital Ltd
36 Chapman Way
Tunbridge Wells
Kent TN2 3EF
enquiries@image-digital.co.uk

ISBN: **978-0-9564237-0-2**

CONTENTS

NOTES

The *stornello* is an Italian short form based around an invocation to a flower. The first line consists of five syllables, the second and third of eleven. The third line is a pay-off to either the person who is the ultimate subject of the poem or, as often in my examples, a thought or consideration. The rhyme scheme is traditionally full/half/full.

Symphonica domestica is my own loose collection of poems that have had a musical origin or inspiration. I have omitted most of the more whimsical or personal ones for this collection.

If dreams are our own

If dreams are our own

Why are we surprised at them?

Their dark surreal stratagem

Paints its vivid cipher zone

And casts you quite alone

With a part at your own requiem.

When dreams are our own

Their fallacious plot and tone

Leave you nothing to condemn

And worse, nothing to condone

Why are we surprised at them?

Autocomphaloscopy

The curtain billows in, the room is cool

The afternoon cobalt is hued by the net-

Like sad music heard after years of retreat

It shocks me to see it again.

A puck of shadow enfolded in crushed flesh,

Sparsely sown with black awkward tuft

Across plump dunes. Thralled, I stretch

Them aside to inspect. And there

Pink and twisted sulks revealed

The knot. I am its balloon.

Hook out the sweaty soaped fluff-

But know well that sick spasm

Tickle when it's touched

And I let it sink back to its sump.

No, this is no way to contemplate

Whoever thought it first couldn't know

The revulsion that prompts any gazer to action.

Look with gratitude out to the garden,

Its fresh banality and beyond.

Cat skull

Have you ever seen a cat skull?

I saw today a thing like a dead sun,

Cold and sunken in a spent white mass.

Blanched and so small,

Kicked by kids and sniffed by dogs

It kept its fragile hollow look

Of a monument-

And like a statue reminded me

Of living times,

The nerve-driven package

We sometimes fuelled on cold days,

Feeling the guilt but irritated still.

Lost, the sad bone lacks the purpose

Its carcass gave it,

A locked pounce in the glistening

Of its hair,

The speed packed and stored through

A lean orange hump

That would shift behind windows,

Filling the room with shadow.

Moth

I saw the brown heart of a moth

Framed in the dawning against the window

I went to write its presence down

To somehow let it go.

None of the pens from the jar would work

Yet I couldn't tell- I had to know

If it sat on the inside or out

Of its silhouette set in the waking glow

So I opened the window into the morning-

Shaken, it plunged to the web below.

I picked a dried pen from the sheath on the table

And unlaced it free to go.

Change

Something had changed

Something had been blown in
Through the window, detritus
Settled leaf-shaped in the angle
Of the tiled wall, cowering
Frail in the brash mustard glare
Flushed over the last water rites.

It would be swept away in the morning,
Part of a cleansing industrious bustle.

Something had shifted

The dark wedge hung still frail
And immobile, near to the dirt-lined
Slits of the ventilator, ready to quiver
In a breath of breeze
Or soft whistled melody.

Pure light crushed through the
Cotton white banner in a drift
Long abandoned as a cobweb
And crisply brushed the nearby wedge.
On its velvet bark was printed
A black ringed eye
And rigid tendrils held it
Firmly to the ceiling.

Something had been said
That made me need to write
Something was alive
That should have been dead.

Just after lights out

Just after lights out and after lights on
I waited under the false August balm
With auras of electric seeping in heaven
And the moon sitting covered, like cavalry restless
Behind the ambush trees and the streetlamp
Taking its share of the sky. But still
I could see the milk drop stars float
In the unclaimed waters of the night Pacific.
Two dead vapours arrowed at the Plough
Caught the last light thrown above.

The flash was a scratch on the eye
A silver flick in the harbour
A skirring sprite across the forest
Abruptly sensed, absorbed,
Never defined. And another
Zipped laughing behind me.

The second night was real, the cloudy
Shutters locked over conversations
And faces from a night sky party
Masking the chatter of the stars indoors.
N o matter, two drops from the shower
Had with streaked fire altered me-
Not from the art of processional fact,
They were quickened jewels in a ring
Perceived from angles and set in the dark-

From what surrounded them they matter now.

Lucifer's riders

In the waft of fat and sugar
From the south-west up the pier
The August bikers stopped their fluid huddle.

Leathers falling down their hips
Motion on their boots a hobble
Unzipped tops betraying modern diet

Clasping helmets, the dark-finned shoal
Sought out the lee behind the arcade
And a solitary girl in flowing gingham.

Off their bikes they looked so fresh
And unlike Lucifer's riders afoot,
All but one with hair trimmed office sharp.

They shuffled, shared theatrical plots,
Turned, demure like girls at parties
Slyly counting glances as approval.

But when the coast grows cold and quiet
They'll split their thighs around their tanks
And roar away to jobs and mother's cooking.

Wheel

They once went out
Painted and dancing
Clutching their spears-
Never questioned the reason
Any more than they
Challenged the season

They never came back.
In the grey and still
Clutching their knees
The other half wondered
At the crude wheel crouched
On the plain, asunder.

Rally

Limbs, head and inside that centre
Hang sweated and heavy from return and rally
From swapping shadows, partners, ends,
From minding the score and chasing the stroke play
Right to left. Let it bounce twice,
The idea that life should creep over the net
And win by default, skid beneath reach
When we know what spins, what happens next,
Stood in a court, all willing and watching.
Let the next first service dream
Beyond the lined images, volley
Patterns played out in different measures-
Which side of the court
Which harmonised hand to arch or sweep
Which homecoming winner to strike before dark?
But here comes the ball.

Some will share love

Some will share love like a child with a song
Form melodies for now with refrains from the past.
Some will love quietly, just humming along.

Many keep silent, they don't yet belong,
Others shout wildly at emotions too vast.
Some will share love like a child with a song.

In the darkness some beat it to sound like a gong
Although screaming inside, afraid it will last.
Some will love quietly, just humming along.

Some sing to the world, (love welcomes a throng),
Many shut eyes and ears, tied to the mast,
Some will share love like a child with a song.

Some will kill love with a ballad too strong
Some will die singing to themselves, outcast.
Some will share love like a child with a song
Some will love quietly, just humming along.

Bluebells under trees

Bluebells under trees

Give way to the madder browns twisting in pairs

Give way to the spring birds rooting in the leaves

Give way to the foxes padding from their lairs

Give way to the summer bees out from the hives

Give way to the roses set for the long term

I will give way to one in the autumn

I never sought to please.

The scent and its velvet hands

The scent and its velvet hands a memory

It's easy to leave a wasted flower

Easier to quit the smelly ripeness of autumn

When the darkness crushes hour on hour

Easiest to tread on the mottled brown plums

Lost from the wounded tree in a shower

But to attend the funeral of spring is hard

The pain fresh as cut flowers from the bower

And the love that would ripen is left in the mind

Its sweetness kept in the sun to sour

Only fuchsias seem to flourish in the shortened light

I shall love only fuchsias from my October tower.

A bouquet of stornelli

Buddleia spray dies
Purple shafts hang spent after six fine days,
Virile quest each year for fewer butterflies.

Bulbs thrust underground,
Left to themselves they tense for Spring in time loaned.
Will you swell with them then from your dark moist mound?

Crocus, first in line
Eager to please, sprouting through lawn for prior gain,
Your lilac against my cold February a sign.

Cyclamen sat cooked
Under the view to the garden newly decked;
But I will keep you tender, not overlooked.

Daffodils return-
Trodden and dug, they bounce back, a circus clown
Playing for love. I'll try to play more than yearn.

Evangeline rose,
Tough climber, you will blossom late as the stars
But each dawn in my garden, love for you grows.

Flowering cyclamen taunt
Easy to crush-beyond arm and eye to paint,
Your soul is so like the flower that it haunts.

Geranium leaves
Display the proud sprayed ring of eternal loves
Each leaf I become, each red flower deceives.

High Norway bluebell
Petals cobalt infused with your lonely will
My blues may also draw the bee to my well.

Lavender heather
Lilac spray sniffed by the world like no other,
You're out of place and time-lets fade together.

Magnolia frost
When the time to emerge with a smile is worst
Your umbrella of silk white dreams will be lost.

Orchid for myself,
The fragrant expense, the curved petals of wealth
Fallen with your memory, brown on the shelf.

Pansies bowed at noon
Black on frocks of red and yellow a frown
Faces deep in thought of darkness come too soon.

Primula, primrose,
One hung in porch casket, one wild between hooves,
I wish I knew which seed in me grows.

Proud thick-skinned yucca
In need of small love, in need of small liquor
If only we needed so little succour.

Red in November
Fuchsias hang in the frost awaiting slumber
Will you feel the cold too, grey by December?

Roses round bower,
Sprung blossoms higher, sharp snaking shafts lower;
Clinger or clung to, who has the last power?

Swaying daffodils
A wave of lithe motion, lemon chorus girls
Conducted from beyond, my fluid windmills.

Wild strawberry, seen
Petite and wary, you cannot be picked full grown
Nor chased clumsily beneath your folds of green.

Your flowers arrive.
Sucking their water, they have something to prove
The love they spread will last, they die but survive.

Always the promise

In a clear cold slide
On the brown shingle pack
I stood to my thighs
In my plastic shoes
Around me the dark brick arch
Let the brook
Cross - purpose
With the solid tracks to London
Bringing timely thunder beats
In well - spaced bouts
And above all that
The power jet's cold war growl
Amplified the thrill
My sense of complete adventure.

Now the net
Is poised behind the shimmer cloak of green
And a sweep
Brings a thudding pile of bolting gudgeon
A smooth brown flicker of a loach
The sparkled dance of an outraged
Stickleback
Always the promise
Of something hiding bright and fast
In the weed.

Clonk

On a beach in a blue August
I would run my hands through
The salted resin of the stones
Banked rippled in tiers,
Filling the blown spaces
Between the splintered lattice works
Of wind-seared breakwater.

At school they said
I was good at throwing things.

There I would set my gallery-
Bent litter, metal flotsam
Lined for glittering dispatch
As I picked the ripest and the best
Granite missiles at my feet.
At my command I would
Execute each stood can,
Felling the row with a threnody
Of forlorn sagging clonks
And a cheer for every death.

At school they said
I was good at throwing things.

Yet I tired of throwing
At a conquered enemy
So I flung the healthiest specimen
Onto the rucked —up carpet of water.
At once it drew the victim
Aloft and down,
Jeering at my marksmanship
In its rhythm, steering
Further away,
Brushing the can's clear
Outline into the general
Green. My shots strayed,
Straddling further and wilder

And I knew with a proud despair
The sea would win.

But at school they said
I was good at throwing things.

With an uncaring arc
I threw a last trajectory
And I knew- never saw-
With a jolt, the clonk.
And the can was wiped away.
I gazed, staggered,
In the gentle screech
Of pebbles sucked by a million straws
And swaggered back
Up the high beach
Past the tar and kelp
To savour my first
Salty sandwich.

Suffice

You were a poet's disappointment,
Rarely raised your flag aloft
In either pithy italics or anointed
In menacing sentiment, though a waft
Could bid our tempers sit up straight
And know their place at the nuclear table.
You'd take your views for a streamlined gait
Down sea-side mews, being fully able
To commune the world's strain through the dog.
Unfashionable, you never slept with your daughter,
Swore at my learning, wore flat cap or clog
And gave studied pignorance no quarter.
No straps, or stubbled jealous boozy wallow
No demand for white shirts or we had it hard
No sitcom fascism or politics to follow;
Only that you asked each side to guard
The suspension bridge that trafficked respect
For others and terriers and things in the woods.
So I'll avoid truffling for gods but expect
Something less to unearth itself and if I could
Just request my own genepool respectfully to splice
Neither ubermann nor beast- a father would suffice.

When I saw the face

When I saw the face it had nothing to say,

It was an island on its cairn of blanket

Sighing in a rhythm of heavy decay

And in the knit of tubes and trinket

A mask, painted puce grey and mottled yellow,

Its base smothered squat-humped in the sheets-

Eighty years of pride made sad and sallow

Trussed and dressed for something incomplete.

Yet in this lump had flown fluttering dissents,

A wheeling flock of loves and grieving,

Their rage, abandonment, sullen comment

Settled now into a flight of leaving,

Orbiting its own life and breath descending

Thick as the mist over loch. And an ending.

We kissed and huskily mouthed goodbye,

The life-giving mottle-faced hump and I.

War and Peace

The shadow curves cool and blue
To me away from the Magnolia tree
And you at the garden table, hot
On the patio blocked in heat and stripe.
The sax from the window sings St Thomas,
The hedge trimmer's strims hot from the right,
Try to cut me out. I feel the blight.
You, reading your big, big book
With your hair up, hidden half
Behind those lilac shafts bursting
From their green and preyed from above
By leering purple tools flared
From the Buddleia. A veering butterfly
Trips, insisting, around my tree
And a myriad of bees and wasps visit
Your colourful bower, your pink top glowering
Over your novel, a girl Appollo.
My eyes cannot read your distant smile,
You cannot gaze beyond my shades.
After a while the shadow bends
Towards you and I am further in.
I try to throw you a pleading look
Watching you read your big, big book.

Near the wall

A voice croaks hollow down the hall
And mingles echoes with the leather,
The frog on the lily pad, near the wall.

Commuters stride on past his call
Too boxed by seconds to worry whether
A voice croaks hollow down the hall.

To tug at sympathy, not to enthral,
His song makes way like a fluttering feather;
The frog on the lily pad, near the wall

Is a threadbare Lucifer in his fall
That best folks flee, at the end of their tether.
A voice croaks hollow down the hall

That's flat as mud, as flat as a drawl,
Incanting plea and gut together,
The frog on the lily pad, near the wall...

'Christ, sing in tune or not at all'
We curse the trains and catch the weather.
A voice croaks hollow down the hall,
The frog on the lily pad, near the wall.

What's new

I like alone

Alone is the new oiled door

Oiled door is the new adventure

Adventure is the new sexual tract

Sexual tract is the new bartering of fact

Bartering of fact is the new relative history

History is the new detachment

Detachment is the new castle

Castle is the new move extended

Extended moves on up to be a well-timed investment

Investment is the new mobility

Mobility is the new evasion

Evasion is the new twist to canny

Canny is the new genes game to survival

Survival is the new intelligence

Intelligence is the new despised elite

Elite is scoring as the new- kitted tribal

Tribal is chanting -'new core esprit!'

Esprit is the new every morning love

Love is the new book on self-regard

Self-regard is the new swivel mirror

Mirror faced is the new alone

Alone is not new

I like alone.

Good idea

My darling could advise *avec plaisir*
Her heart was good, her intentions sincere
That's why the refrain rang in my ear...
'Don't you think it's a good idea
If...'

My sense of style was not this year
Her ex had much more sense of gear
So buy some stuff, impress your peer
'Don't you think it's a good idea
If...'

The larder is full; it's safe from here
A sense of pleasure taken draws near-
But from the shadows, a little more austere,
'Don't you think it's a good idea
If...'

'Your belly balloons, it's too much beer,
I know a diet to which you could adhere
And reduce that wobble around your rear
Don't you think it's a good idea
If...'

Alas she must go - that much was clear
So how to do it, which path to steer?
But what is that whisper in the wind I hear-
'Don't you think it's a good idea
If...'

The task is done, the road is clear
To save my life and improve my career
But how to get rid of your body my dear?
'Well - don't you think it's a good idea
If...'

Grey

Grey is the undertone of face and shape
Our favourite limpid colour
We put it forward as our candidate
Every day

Grey is our cover, cleaner in half-tone
An exchange of national values
Painting the absolutes of vivid behaviour
In our nice way.

Grey is the understanding coming by night
Reduced in shadowed anger
To survey the day of where we are going-
It makes the heart stay.

Grey is the inner shades of black and white
The kindness of second thoughts,
The hand that opts to put the gun on the table
And feels that way.

Grey is the power of androgyny
The content of no fixed place
It knows the logic, feels the reason
Of might and may.

Grey is beholden to nothing of the moment
The sea in February,
Its heat sucked from the saturation of life
A hued delay.

All are welcome

Now the purpose that people were invited to church-

When its meaning had erstwhile been left in the lurch-

Was to go at the nugget of words with a knife

And to somehow cut out the whole meaning of life.

It brought lots of earnest grey people in glasses

And sensible clothes from the frumpier classes

To harass the Word long and hard with their woes

And discover just where that mean life-purport flows.

Sit down and talk and discover right here-

All are welcome, whatever from childhood you fear,

You can talk to your neighbour, look under the chair,

But the bastard of life won't be meaning right there,

Not our meaning, it's slippier than your lavender soap

And life's purpose is guessed at by microscope;

Its purpose is to make you feel warm in your clothes

Whose meaning is to make you feel cool. So it goes.

Cast around

Life is a little like fishing

A cast in the lake and you wait-

Nothing doing, you've used the wrong bait

And caught nothing with cursing and wishing.

Next up much swirling and swishing

With various ploys up to date-

But life is quite like fishing

A cast in the lake and you wait.

Eons on and you feel like dishing

Up poison to the fish that you hate

For leaving you wet and squishing.

Life is a hundred percent like fishing

A cast in the lake and you wait.

At last

The dream of a love

The meeting of the known and the unexpected

Brought to a soul made too late

So like

A sparrow at last in the hedgerow

Singing late in November

 A butterfly flouting its wings

Against the autumn frost

Sipping from a lukewarm cup

 Left hurriedly

Back in the early morning

The dying fantasy of Christmas

Recharged each year at a growing distance

The fields and streams revisited

That led your feet to school

Where the new houses now stand...

...The laugh of a girl I should have known

Long before I walked away.

You will never see

You will never see the play from theatre's plush illusion

Never stroke the textures from a printed catalogue

Never know the story from the terse conclusion

Or sense the machinations from one cog.

Impossible to tread mapped journeys from a plane

Likewise to sail blind in a dove-grey mist

Hopeless to wade the rivers from a frantic train

Impossible to gauge the peaks in their clouded fist

You cannot guess the black depths from the waves

You cannot live lost lives read from cold graves

You cannot walk the world before the door

You cannot hear the music from the score

You cannot see my love from where you are,

Its world, its colours or its passionate vista.

Cloak

I don't like woman writers much
They scuff the world, not profound as such.
I don't like men unless they're French
And love me with indifference.
I prefer the café bonhomie
Of Provence to most of humanity.
I stand aside and tot up lines
Which stretch up naked, then recline
And drawl out taunts in time to dine.
The syllables I suck are my caress
The mire I plough and then undress,
Though cloaked myself is how I feel free.
You will have guessed
That I write poetry.

I collect the close range dirty guilt
And mix it with my own good silt
I source and scan the useful droves, hence
The cute retelling of 'experience'.
One or two novels will also come
About people I've screwed up (Wasn't that fun)
But for now the characters lie in rows
My verse is rifling through their prose
And the words are maggots on their meat-
They're dead like cowboys in the street.
Life's an epicure of iambics and brie
Awards and rewards from the detritus and scree
Will cover my feet
When I write poetry.

Shift

I declare

I was aground

On a sandbank

That never used to be there.

I looked down

Through the water

And the sands were

Grains

Piles of grains

That came together

Again

In a different place

And a different shape

According to the tide race

And the grains

Were all the people

Who under the sea

Were there to disagree

With me.

Symphonica Domestica

(Extracts)

Boheme

Musetta chirped her waltz with no bass
And little top from the shelf
You whistled discretely from the kitchen
Exactly a fourth out all the way.
That is how you kept your mission-
Out but perfectly pitched with yourself.

No 4 in C – The 'Domestic'

I am being unfaithful darling
Unfaithful, daring in my way
Being faithful to my lack of faith
And doing it best I can every day

I'm at it when you make the tea
I'm at it when you drive
I'm at it when you smile at me
I'm at it when you swive.
And as for other women
Yes I've had them up to where
My belt gets tighter every year
Much tighter than I care
To tell this truth; well - pitch at it
I'm trying to have an affair
Through babble and cacophony
That is, the one past interruptus
With headphones and with symphonies
Where I play with myself at conductors.

Wedding Choir

We were happy to sing and steer a flow
Of tune and verse that we were taught
And even now their sound outweighs the blame
For failure that a little knowing brought their way.
Belief and system, knots and vows survive
In caves away from the ice-age in white coats
And if the old is lost on maps of dead roads
Or warmed by fire that's painted, still a younger
Anger loves its coarse retreat, a prouder
L'homme arme. The God we hate and crave
Has moved on out to a further smear of stars
And no doubt contemplates a re-design,
A what-to-do and how to spark a second time
Some tinsel speck in the balloon of dead creation.

Well love isn't Jazz

If love was Jazz
I'd be pummelled at leisure
Scarred by its frisson
And its ramrod pleasure.

If love was a trombone
It would be push and pull too soon
Then everything's on the slide
Using position to stay in tune.

If love was a set of drums
It would only give me stick
And I'd beg for a better melody
(And harmony). Beat it quick.

If love became a trumpet
Then I'd only stick my mellow
Fingers in my ears
And my face into a pillow.

If love was a tenor horn
I'd beg it to stop talking,
Stop admiring its own jokes
And its narcissistic squawking.

If love was a guitar
I'd say play with me and adapt
Instead of plucking with yourself
And your super leather straps.

Miles and Trane
Could hawk the talk
About love and the doo da da
But they could only tap my toe
When Johann led my soul
Onto go and took it fa fa fa.

So don't delude
About Bach and his prelude
The trouble with music as love
-Do you hear-
Is that you have to listen
And brush your ears
Not close them down
To the beat beat beat
Of Jazz repeat repeat repeat..

Repertoire

With fragments held in the fingers
Paint the aura with training of the eye
As sky about their restless silhouettes.
Play till understanding fills your portrait
Or hope that its sketch
Will impress across the wind.

Dance To The Music

Slinky Eros in deadening age
Is a charity dressing up
In formal dancing clothes
Jiving badly to old tunes.
A freedom is announced
But faulty with its spelling,
In a room where the mirrors
Should be blackened not reversed,
If it all comes at last
Down to seeking the other.

New Quartet- Analysis

Tributaries silting meet and flow
Milk and dark towards an ocean,
A pair of mirrored chants goes curdling.

Two snakes mating, two birds circling
Two, forever two-time snared
In jagged passionate call, in melody.

Glide of meld, clash and resonance
Deep to top, cello to fiddle.
And then a seep of notes. A third one.

Quiet, but growing fast to master
From the centre, singing and saying
So much with a little bow and range.

The trio hatches. With honey burnish
Viola broadens the joy, perks
The argument flutters, vying for place.

The chamber warms with dissent, suspensions,
Flights off the stave and coloured persuasions,
The domicile harmony at its ripest.

Its work is done, a wine rich balanced
Sound of reason, rush of fancy
Modern thorn, branches of taste.

Then a wonder. Sounds of two are gone.
The warmth is gutted, the duet flows on
Slower, broader, the old themes sadder

Until a cadence breaks the tune.
Lone and unsure, winding a threnody,
The violin knits a puzzled cadenza.

Artemis unbound

The case slipped back.
Its curved trunk yielding
Twenty years waiting
Coiled silver ochre
Barely burnished,
Tubes curled into
Mainline and branches
Twisted and knitted
Around themselves,
The pistons sitting
On the nodes of direction.

He took the silver
Funnel and blew
And then in a sound
Stood his friend again his voice
Between bursts a Glasgow
Bronze of security
And me agog
As a child just hearing.
Then I was walking

Across the beach
Swinging and marching,
Singing the second
Under his first
In the parallel past
Of Brandenburg
That waited for mastery
Like his long ago.

And then it stopped.
The present voice said
It would fetch a fair price
At Paxmans with care.
And so it returned
To its velvet, no longer
A dead skull bound
In its coffin but now
A fanfare of hunting,
Hidden, still ringing
Around its golden
Waking sound of
Rejuvenation.

A Desperate Cry

Maybe the little man balding
Will knock by again sharp
And gem-eyed, lapping at the door
With a pamphlet on tones and rows
And the old true way at the lintel-
Maybe we will pick one from the sheaf
To read it through before tea
Smile, nod and mouth the cadences
Whilst he will go hot and smart
Down the road, whistling a tune
The one left over in C major.

Repton

Down the corridor a rising fifth
Struck intimate in the heroic key,
Not some theme from a granite slab symphony,
Just a hymn for the morning.

It was tentative, halting, dissonant, misplaced,
The girls were laughing but found themselves crooning
In low stubborn accord. Then suddenly
The four -square fervour picked up its stays
And in a mist lightly stepped on my childhood
Waking naves and stalls and evensong,
Coarse congregations, white faces on cassocks,
Drifting unsung for three decades until
Tripping at last on a ready coffin,
Just a hymn for the mourning.

So now a new luminosity chokes
And glows for me, propelled by memory,
The barest beauty of broken sound,
And the girls are laughing, yet unwound sing
Compelled, loving the license it brings.

Brought down

Though he brought it down from heaven
God died when he was twenty seven-
Though it brought us down to earth
Still we don't know what the music's worth.

New 100th

They used to boast walkie - talkie
Now their shrivelled feet can shuffle nowhere
And their voices say nothing out loud
But commune up and down in their hair.

They take virtual pride in their ur-sons
All sat at their educate-nodes,
Trace the path of their genetic daughters
Carving wealth paths at career-base cathodes.

All people where on earth do they dwell,
Are they trimmed and rationed
Slimmed and fashioned without smell
Seeking comforts and loves
In the airtight hell?

At the neural screens
For three units a time
No need to get testy
All are sculpted in their prime.

The fat ones are gone
The bad ones are dead
The old ones are paid
To keep quiet in my head.

And along came Mozart

And along came Mozart
Mozart waiting in the wings
Just add celluloid
Mozart in the zeitgeist
Mozart and Pimms
Make that Mozart o'clock
Mozart in the *fin de siècle*
Haydn femme de Mozart
Mozart fin de Beethoven
Mozart good for your babies
Dark chocolate Mozart
Good for your heart every day
Mozart in spas
In the Wells
In the malls
Size eight Mozart
A little light music
Yves Klein Nachtmusik
The Three Mozarts
With a box of truffles
On a smooth Sunday morning.
You know when you've been Wolfied.

Andante

The steps of slow music
Make a sadder walk
Towards and away-
The melody and beat
As I listen right here
Animate the stories there
In faces and voices
And vague places in time.
It can mould hot reveries,
Reshape with tidal sounds
All emotion, all colours
In regrets and evasions
Or rework the myths
To a happier end.
But most of all it squeezes
From me acid drop tears.
The ghost are staying young
And walking away.

Storm

Filled in a corner
Spilt blood of fear,
Lightning tears away
To see where you are
In the night.
A touch of scary
To be bathed in blue-
Cover yourself
In dangerous pity
The foetal delight
Must never come out.
And the waves of noise
Recede in space
Leaving a drip
Of wet pleasure
Safe as you are
In your dark chocolate place.

Leavers photo

An envy of their voyage

Is what it comes to now,

Sullen before their assemblage

Of smiles in the local gazette;

A convoy that will scatter,

Pushed by wolves of ambition,

Contrition and social matter,

But for now they silently wave

To me, their static pier master,

Leaving their bottles and chocolates

And their knife-shafts of youth and disaster.

Spitfire

Not really such a bloody stupid name

Men must have felt they could easily be wedded

To this thing- their souls aflame

To stroke her fiery controls; and that beds

The virgin hovering question – she or it?

Her vamp off that narrow entrance high

To low is no place for brute testament, split

Now in a musky turn that spreads its bridal

Veils to reveal two perfect oval thighs.

Some would say a cool angel of Lucifer

For hire, looking over her shoulder

Down at us, burning the sluice of

Cloud in eights and zero, colder

Curves autograph the hot low

Sky, underlined in final pass

Before slipping her panties in a slow

Slow blush to relieve herself on the grass.

Ein feste burg

High on the harbour the squares of stone

Spread round to guard the last great tower

Its swathes of needless grass new mown

To brush the carpet for the visiting hour;

Its purpose then and its duty in time

Is a couplet of laughter in history's rhyme.

Children dance on its cannoned wall

Shouting brute things in response and call

The sense of loss and gain is overpowering.

Dead in the wilderness

A problem shared

Is a problem released

From safe captivity

As a vulnerable beast.

Once you invite them

Friends will always feed

Like concerned buzzards

On your carcass of need.

The friend who likes to beg the question

The friend who solves it over digestion

The friend who steers it into congestion

The friend who always makes a suggestion.

The problem you share

Is dead in the wilderness,

Hunted, picked at,

Sickly, bare.

That man

That man on the seat
Is playing a song of abundance
Alone to the mantle
Around him of redundance

He has shaken the twelve
Tone expected of life
And stayed with melody
Of one line his wife

He wears the crooked bag
Into which his good looks
Were placed to make room
For the freedom of books

He commands the pen
Into which the sheep sex
Has been driven grateful
By his faithful dog text

He is fat and young ugly
He splays bold and red
He dreams of writing down
Many things in his head

Can he be a man
Has he no erection?
No better than that
He can exist on affection.

Concern

When you called me
A wise old bird
My feathers shivered a little
Even as my keen eyes shone.
A bald lined neck is ballast
For many things known
But all I gave you was a
Cynicism disguised as
Concern, jealousy disguised
As direction. And then,
Did I want to be old or wise?
I'd gladly go solo
And empty-headed
Reaching for the canopy
And gaunt face crag,
Picking up bits of nature
To bind them again without
Quite knowing why...
But I thank you for your compliment
Of distant love,
To where I once could fly.

The soft music

The rain beats a thwarted pummel
In slant across the window
Your absence is louder at the door
And drips singing over the roof
I will hear its cold song tonight
Even in the woody warmth
As I stare out

It holds my head
Breaks my eye line
Drowns the soft music
Of my choice

The glade

Supple, exotic in lilac

Your dancer's limbs

Burst through the dark held canopy

And your petal red mouth

Sings for a sunlit glade in my week

Before you close the dark branches

Behind you again.

You still flower

But the heart you have left

Without hearing its song

Turns to long parched

Dry laments of waiting.

Last Leaf

You are the last leaf on my tree
Stay- stay as long as you can
Fluttering your breast and waist
With an oriental graceful sway
For me in metre and rhyme
Stay as long as you can in this place-
All the prettiest leaves fall in time.

My own Einstein

I am my own Einstein after fifty years

The word relativity looms as older age nears

Each love grows in distance as time expands

Until the memory stops running, shakes, and stands

Just staring, waiting for the hours to contract

In a fairytale or science fiction final act

When the space warp finds a node behind

The time you started from- a story kind

In heart, ignoring the mirror and chemical collapse

And the possibility of learning from it all, a lapse

Of sense as well as perspective.

The reality of loss is a hard corrective.

Yet each of my loves gained more and more

Wrapped like Russian dolls, keeping the one before

Or a series of ever-growing love nets thrown

Gathering all the sadness of the last I had known.

Four hands

These hands can play the tempos of feeling
Spinning their rondo planes of movement.

The hour hand measures nothing read
Its transit offers discoveries at points
Of difference-one-two –never-
Birthday, Christmas, life is forever.
It is the hand of my childhood days
And precious with its ignorance of change.

The minute hand surprises us
Glance away and back and things have moved
It beckons ambition, the drive in its measures
Says time is bountiful, build on its pleasures.
It is the hand of my middle age
And precious with its awareness of change.

The second hand quickens, fast as it sounds
Each stiff click a mocking- a beat of
Infinite panic-a tread that scoffs
And weeps at once – a dark crossing off.
It is the hand of my old age
And precious with its hatred of change.

And there the last hand squats at seven
Like a spider noticed on the wall
It says the days are not mine-or yours-
The hands glide round its throne of hours.
It is the hand of day after day
Its value I cannot measure.

A certain time

After a certain time,

Never defined, always divined,

And felt as a grey sublime,

You spend not mend

Earn not learn

Spy not sigh

Rant not pant

Hint not sprint

Get not bet

Deal not feel

Covet not love it

And after the recognition

You know the condition

By all that you aren't

Or can't.